HYPEROPIA JUSTICE

A Criminal Justice Paradox of Unfair Prison Sentencing and Early Exposure to Social Disparities

Tisha S. Arther

HYPEROPIA JUSTICE

A Criminal Justice Paradox of Unfair Prison Sentencing and Early Exposure to Social Disparities

Dedication

I would like to dedicate this book to my late father, Zeke Parker Jr. II. You were more than great. You gave me the strength to keep trying even when things got hard. I miss you. I love you, daddy.

Contents

Preface
What is the trajectory for your life?

Raising up youth for the way of the world seems surreal. It is important that many of us not only understand the disparities in the criminal justice system, but find ways we can improve it. The goal of my book is to uncover topics that are interrelated within the criminal justice disciplinary to promote the erudition of an ultimately broken system. When looking beyond what is presented before the eye, some struggle to see fine details that help impair how justice is served unto disadvantaged others. Furthermore, they develop a case of hyperopia, in which they are blinded by nescient distortions of America's detrimental criminal justice reform occurring before them.

Studying criminology is very complex. As a two-time graduate of Saint Leo University, I have ascertained so much information regarding the rule-makers, the lawbreakers, and the social institutions responsible for creating injustice. If I were to do anything with this newly attained knowledge, it would be to educate our society on how the justice system works for a certain group of people. It is important that society understand contributing factors to injustice in the criminal justice system. It is also vital to beware of how social construct can transform the way laws are implemented. Moreover, highlighting the laws that are in favor of those with wealth and of the majority, which keeps minorities oppressed.

If I can articulate in a way that the average human being can understand and acknowledge the need for reformed criminal justice, we can contribute to sanguine ideas to help improve racial and socio-economic equality in the American criminal justice system. This book is a combination of research that I have ascertained in my studies of criminal justice.

Introduction

Drug possession laws in the state of Virginia are strict and specifically driven. When inquiring upon drug laws in the state of Virginia, it was discovered that a person does not have to have drugs on their person to be criminally charged with possession. Instead, it must be in a person's oversight. If a person can physically reach the drugs, it is considered to be within their leverage. And even if the person cannot ascertain the drugs, if the drugs are in a place only that person has direct access to, they can also be charged. The problem here suggests that unfair prison sentences are judgments that can be permanent and harsh for non-violent offenders by way of mandatory minimum sentencing. Tough drug laws disproportionately affect arrests of minorities who fall victim to mass incarceration. Just imagine, a small number of drugs can land a person of color a lengthy prison sentence, especially if it is not a first-time offense, and drug possession is the right classification; for example, Schedule I drugs. Should an offender who was caught with drug possession more than twice (three-strikes) be serving the same maximum prison sentence as a murderer?

It can be assumed that the criminal justice system has two faces: the criminal justice system for the elite and prominent, and the criminal justice system for the marginalized and disadvantaged. The assumption can also be made that due to unfair prison sentencing, the overall population of America's prison system is devastatingly disadvantaged. This book expounds upon the factors related to the harms of unfair sentencing in criminal justice. Throughout my research, the ascertainment of eight mitigating factors are delineated in such a way to contribute to the discussion of how unfair sentencing plagues communities, webbed within a dark cycle of institutionalized racism.

Factors

First, one must expound upon the factors related to the harms of unfair sentencing in criminal justice. Through this section, one will ascertain a delineation of eight factors contributing to how unfair sentencing dampers communities.

- **Factor One:** Stereotypes enforces unfair sentencing. America's drug epidemic enforced the stereotypical portrayal by the media to inflict mandatory minimum sentencing and no-knock warrants on people of color.

- **Factor Two:** Mass incarceration of a drug crime will not cease from unfair prison sentencing due to ongoing societal strain. Although America's prison system has the trajectory of deterring crime, private prisons require cheap prison labor, and unfair prison sentences continue to daunt impoverished communities.

- **Factor Three:** There are collateral damages from the consequences of receiving an unfair sentence. Those once incarcerated can never move past the stigma attached to their convictions.

- **Factor Four:** Mass incarceration is a form of social control. A public that encourages punitive action is a determinant of weakened criminal justice reform.

- **Factor Five:** Black women are included in the racial discrimination shown by some law enforcement officers. Black women fear that if they are stopped by the police, they will not see a day of trial.

- **Factor Six:** When Black Americans kill law enforcement officers, they will be sentenced to death. However, when officers shoot and kill unarmed Black Americans, these same consequences are not reciprocated.

- **Factor Seven:** The school-to-prison pipeline gives children of color early exposure to unjust prison sentencing. The lack of law enforcement officer training causes problems in school settings. Also, the lack of parental supervision and education influences disproportionate minority contact (DMC).

- **Factor Eight:** Interviewing and interrogation practices used on adults should not be used on minors or those with mental health disabilities. The Reid technique that some officers use to question suspects is problematic and is not effective on youth or people with mental health disabilities.

Part One:
Stereotypes Excuse Unfair Sentencing

"We, the police, find the defendant guilty," says no law enforcement agency ever. However, stereotypes perpetuated by the majority explain ongoing suspicion, which has turned into a manifestation of proactive police measures. This, promotes massive police encounters that lead to the enforcement of unfair sentencing within a demographic in both large or small communities. The first encounters of the criminal justice system start with the experience of local law enforcement officers.

Not all law enforcement officers act upon stereotypes while serving large or small communities, but when it happens, it strikes hard. With surveillance and proactive contacts, law enforcement officers have saturated many communities (Geller & Fagan, 2019). Surveillance and proactive engagements includes a torpedo of racial tension heavily armed on Black American and Latino communities by racial profiling, officer pressure, officer harassment, occurrences of stop and frisk, and the selectivity of enforcing laws that impact the way officers enforce drug laws (Rosino & Hughey, 2018). Today, nearly everyone has access to a cellular phone, helpful in recording injustices that people of color have always experienced.

Let's examine questionable saturation with the enforcement of drug laws. America's racist stereotypes and fears about the negative outlook on minorities are tied to drug laws with the common misconception that poor people of color commit drug crimes (Rosino & Hughey, 2018). How are Black Americans disproportionately targeted in unjust sentencing? Black Americans are targets in a socioeconomic context in bail and pretrial detention (Hood & Schneider, 2019).

The moral panic that created a framework that produced mass incarceration and oppression in America is an unceasing problem even when magnified. Considering there are excessive amounts of imprisoned people due to strict laws and policies, the war on drugs has something to do specifically with the marginalized who are standardized and placed in connection to the drugs, not the legitimacy of the drugs themselves. Roughly 95,000 Black men are in federal prison (Rehavi & Starr, 2014). Black Americans and Latinos are linked in connection to drugs as a way to discredit, devastate, and demoralize their communities.

Imagine, racial minorities represent about 37 percent of the population in America; however, they make up over 60 percent of the incarcerated population (Jackson et al., 2015). Additionally, Jackson et al. (2015) posits the abundance of such individuals incarcerated is linked to the polices targeting the sale, manufacture, distribution, and use of drugs, which has socioeconomically disadvantaged communities by disrupting families.

Black American males are misrepresented in the news and are also portrayed as criminals, more than White Americans (Hurley et al., 2015). Furthermore, Hurley et al. (2015) asserts support for law enforcement officers is affected by stereotypical news coverage that connects Black Americans disproportionately to criminal activity. Therefore, stereotypical news associations expose blackness and criminality, while Whites may fight for more stringent criminal justice laws and policies based on these arbitrary associations. Rehavi & Starr (2014) posits lengthy prison sentences cemented in federal districts customarily held in place for Blacks.

How does one pinpoint where the inconsistency lies in sentencing discrepancies unsolved? For starters, the mandatory minimum sentencing occurs systematically and exposes sentencing inequalities embedded within institutionalized racism (Rehavi & Starr, 2014). Stereotypes have a linkage to cognitive memory. When blackness and criminality are somehow linked together by stereotypical news, policies become based on these preconceived attributions (Hurley et al., 2015). Consequently, there is a significant difference between races in how the criminal justice system is perceived (Mondak et al., 2017). Black and Whites generally have different perceptions of how the law works for them, with Blacks having a more negative outlook on law enforcement.

Why do Black Americans face more mandatory minimum sentencing than White Americans? Imagine not only being unfairly targeted by law enforcement on the profile biases of the race, but combine with that the practice of exercising subtle prosecutorial discretion. Prosecutorial discretion allows for liberal sentencing power for selective offenses (Rehavi & Starr, 2014). Leniency is problematic and can explain disparities amongst the color lines of the incarcerated. Mandatory minimum sentencing has a positive correlation to unfair sentencing and blackness. The way that prosecutors choose to charge cases becomes significant in discovering inequalities. If an offender is Black, male, and a federal arrestee, there is a chance that they may face a lengthier prison sentence than a White offender for the same crimes, and with the same priors. Mandatory minimum sentencing becomes a grave concern. Moreover, many of the racial disparities that are founded by the type of offense and the offenders' advances are explained by the initial decision that the prosecutors make to file charges, which possess a mandatory minimum sentence (Rehavi & Starr, 2014).

The federal prosecutor should not overlook details when examining disparity risks involving sentencing, but they do. Prosecutors utilize a great deal of discretion in deciding how to charge defendants and deciding if a plea deal will be accepted. This, directly affects the length of time offenders will serve behind prison walls (Kovera, 2019). Unlike judges, prosecutors are required to justify leniency when they utilize discretion and their decisions are not reviewed by the power of a higher court (Fischman & Schanzenback, 2012). On the other hand, prosecutors possess very cogent reasons to oppose capital appeals that keep them away from winning, and that are also likely to further their political vocations (Jacobs et al., 2007). Another contributor to the risk of an offender being wrongfully convicted is having an inexperienced as a prosecutor. When prosecutors start their careers, all defendants represent the 'bad guys' and law enforcement officers seem to be righteous (Levine & Wright, 2017).

Mandatory minimum sentences derive from stereotypes. A highlighted societal problem, like drug abuse, sounds the alarm for public fear. Baranauskas & Drakulich (2018) suggest that the way the public understands the problem and the potential solutions to the problems is critical. To connect a crime to an entire race is faulty and has long-term socio-economic consequences. Therefore, stereotypes derived from an identifiable crime are objectively unexplainable. There are inconsistencies between public perception and the reality of evil, primarily if the public is receiving information solely from media influence. The news media may not be the sole media source for the crime. Depending on where a person resides and who has residency in the community, corruption should not be overestimated. For example, if a White American is living in a city where there is a large population of Black Americans, they may be inclined to link being Black with the crime after viewing news reports (Baranauskas & Drakulich, 2018).

Part Two:
America's Incarceration Problem Will Not Solve Drug Problems

The cat is no longer in the bag; the Land of the Free has an incarceration problem. Furthermore, this problem will not deter drug crimes but create other societal dilemmas. Drugs are problematic even despite mandatory minimum sentences such as three-strike laws. The United States incarceration rate is so systematic, with over 2 million offenders, and the vast majority will be released back into society (Turney & Schneider, 2016). So then, what is the problem? Incarceration views permanent crime solutions as locking an offender up and throwing away the key. The trajectory should utilize punishment as a deterrent and rehabilitative tool. Goals for the prison system are often competitive and conflict with corrections facing challenges, such as broader societal implications and prison shortfalls. Other impositions include the aging prison population, more female inmates, mental health, high financial costs of corrections, size and capacity, prison workforce challenges, recidivism, and changing technology (Jackson et al., 2015).

The offenders who are behind bars are human beings, too; however, society has lost sight of that due to public fear, moral panic, and public perception. The reality is that inmates are aging in prison. Moreover, there is convincing evidence indication that individuals grow out of crime (Gottschalk, 2011). Not only is there an increase in inmates serving life in prison, but approximately 16 percent of the national prison population is 50 years of age and older (Jackson et al., 2015). America's prisons also house offenders with life-long mental health issues. Both aging inmates and those who are mentally ill are rather costly. Therefore, the problem that the war on drugs attempted to solve created a whole plethora of other obstacles. Meanwhile, there is still a drug problem outside of corrections.

How does lengthy and unjust sentencing deter America's drug problem? Mass incarceration on drug crimes is a definitive result of punitive anti-drug policies that the war on drugs previously initiated. Moreover, the evidence for the success rate of imprisonment in deterring drug use is quite questionable. Reduction in recidivism is unlikely if prison sentences are not linked with drug treatment (Mitchell et al., 2017). Incarceration often increases drug use among drug offenders and makes way for networking capabilities with other drug offenders (Roberts & Yu Chen, 2013).

What drives America's prison problem? Private prisons. For-profit prisons decrepitating criminal justice reform is a relevant factor to the incarceration problem. Boyle & Stanley (2019) helps examine human rights violations inside of prisons as a way to challenge the legitimacy of private prisons. Any business that gets rich from the backs of the incarcerated supports mass incarceration.

Opportunity for shareholders to establish wealth from prison labor contributes to inhumane treatment of prisoners. Nevertheless, as some members of society may posit, prisons are supposed to be unpleasant, not a desirable place to be. One must examine closely every underlying problem. Private prisons help keep prisons full because it is cost-effective for them. Selman & Leighton (2010) suggests that as more companies generate revenue from corrections, there is a chance of misusing power within the multi-million-dollar business, leading to distorted sentencing policies, the goal of which is profit. Therefore, the outcome is that each offender serves a lengthy sentence behind bars.

Not only are private prisons politically driven, but they do not solve the real socioeconomic problems. Mack, Jones & Ballesteros (2017) delineates how drug use and drug overdoses continue to reflect critical public health challenges. Unfortunately, in the US, drug problems are treated as criminal offenses as opposed to an arena of complicated health-related challenges. The problem further ratiocinates the leading cause of injury death in America, claiming approximately 52 thousand deaths in 2015 by drug overdose (Mack, Jones & Ballesteros, 2017). More drug-related deaths will meet America's incarceration problem if the only solution to ending the war on drugs is handled by way of mass incarceration and unjust sentences for non-violent minority offenders.

This section will definitively ratiocinate why individuals engage in drug crimes and delineate how harsher sentences for Black Americans are due to societal strains encountered as a community. A great portion of the American population is involved with the correctional system, approximately one in 35 people (Jackson et al., 2015). Social and cultural factors linking strain and stressors to drug crimes are significant. Everyone wants a slice of the pie, but not everyone has the same advantages. Not to mention, individuals respond to strains in various ways. Furthermore, when law enforcement officers target a specific racial or ethnic group due to suspicion, there is a lack of trust established. Unfortunately, victimization is likely due to the socialization of drug behaviors in impoverished communities that house like-minded individuals, making them more vulnerable targets (Iratzoqui, 2018).

Poor treatment can result in further crime. It is recognized that in poorer Black American and Latino communities, law enforcement officers serve primarily to monitor and subjugate rather than to serve and protect, resulting in deep resentment as well as radical, oppositional awareness (Rickford, 2016). This poor treatment has an affiliation with those who have low social control, and having low social control is a strain. Strains in impoverished communities create not only hostility, but it may allow individuals to mitigate these strains by turning to drugs. Some strains include but are not limited to unemployment, mental health problems, single-parent households, poverty, lack of education, which drives the excuse given for the mass incarceration of Blacks and Latinos, and as well as other forms of institutionalized racism. Some individuals lack the proper resources to deal with societal strains; therefore, they have very little to lose by turning to drugs.

Irattzoqui (2018) posits how drug crimes are an effective way of regaining control and ascertaining some semblancy of power after experiencing victimization. Inequality has cemented the roots of the incarceration problem in America. Furthermore, as long as America uphold stereotypes, Black Americans and Latinos will continue to face mass incarceration and unfair sentencing stemming from the societal strain experienced by both marginalized groups. Parker, Stults & Rice (2005) found that increased levels of disadvantage among Black Americans deepen racial group differences, making them more observable, which leads to increased social control against poor Blacks in the form of incarceration.

Part Three:
The Collateral Damage from Mass Incarceration

Despite enduring criminal records in Virginia, the collateral consequences of mass incarceration of minorities include losing the right to vote, loosing child custody, and deportation. Many offenders are also punished through the federal lifetime ban on public assistance (Yang, 2017). Mass incarceration has real-life consequences: Family structures and social bonds are weakened by legal confinement, which inhibits the emotional and psychological development of minority youth, increasing the economic instability households may have (Harris, 2015).

Collateral damage also occurs when ex-offenders who are men have limited employment opportunities. Consequently, any chance of a stable family foundation, maintaining stability, or even finding a life partner is challenging. An individual's upbringing additionally sets the tone for being a victim of collateral consequences. Harris (2015) further implies that incarceration is intergenerational, a person can be either the offender or parents of the offender, both depicts a culture of incarceration.

When offenders exit the incarceration process, there may be other consequences faced, even after offenders have served their time. Zinger (2012) suggests that parole was implemented as a plausible step in the overall correctional process, specifically to assist the reintegration of offenders into the community as law-abiding citizens. However, collateral damage follows inmates outside prison walls when trying to turn a new leaf and overcome adversity. For example, in some states, there is a lifetime ban on public assistance. Ex-offenders convicted of a state or federal charge for drugs are definitively banned by The Personal Responsibility and Work Opportunity Reconciliation Act of

1996 (Paresky, 2017). Some states opted out of the lifetime band and required the compliance of other restrictions. These particular states also recognize how banning ex-offenders from public assistance will increase recidivism due to economic reasons. Different states have laws that enforce ex-offenders ascertain drug treatment and testing for public assistance eligibility (Mondack et al., 2017). The state of Virginia revokes driver's licenses for non-motor vehicle drug charges, making it difficult for ex-offenders to commute to and from employment. When ex-offenders have the tools or benefits that will help them economically, they genuinely have a chance at a clean slate.

To further ratiocinate about collateral damage from mass incarceration, the arrest and later suicide of Kalief Browder is an example of collateral damage stemming from unjust sentencing and racial discrimination. Jones (2016) posits how structural violence entails poverty and institutionalized racism in which the justice system engages in systemic denials of civil liberties. Moreover, Jones explains how structural violence exists because society fails to recognize it. Suspected of being an assailant for a robbery, he was arrested based on suspicion and the fact that this was not Browder's first run-in with the law. He was incarcerated, waiting three years for his trial because of social class.

Poverty and institutionalized racism kept Browder from making bail. Jones also believed that the criminal justice system indirectly killed Browder due to the fostering of a justice system that houses defendants, detaining them for years without trial, leaving them little hope for the future. Imagine the failure to see an individual as a human being, what Jones calls a social death by barbarically holding human beings never convicted of a crime. Browder was a casualty of systematic racism that kept heaps of dark clouds over disadvantaged Black Americans and Latinos (Jones, 2016).

The significance of Browder's imprisonment and death suggests that there are arrests that occur unevenly across racial lines. The ability to meet bail is pre-determined by class, and pretrial detention is likely to have insidious consequences for the offender and their families who face an abundance of inequalities (Hood & Schneider, 2019). The 8th Amendment enforces the Excessive Bail Clause to ensure that offenders can make bail. They have the ability to remain free until a jury finds them guilty at trial. However, many offenders cannot post bail, which signifies no pretrial freedom (Woodruff, 2013). Black Americans are concentrated in impoverished urban areas that have limited access to employment networks and opportunities to be marketable (Parker, Stults & Rice, 2005).

There are psychological aspects of being incarcerated. Ex-offenders witness and experience things outsiders would only see on television, or if they have been inside prison walls themselves. The consequences exacerbated by lengthy sentencing includes social introversion, institutionalization, distrust, psychological distancing, suicidal tendencies, and depression (Munn, 2011). Ewing (2016) posits 30 percent of offenders in solitary confinement have a mental illness. Moreover, exposure to an extreme environment, such as incarceration, brings challenges post-carceral.

Not only does mass incarceration and a lengthy sentence have dire collateral consequences for the ex-offender, but the children that they left behind. Turney & Schneider (2016) examines the collateral consequences of incarceration for men. They show an association between incarceration history from the father and the father's contribution to their households. Turney & Schneider was able to reflect on how mass incarceration perpetuates a wealth inequality. Furthermore, the time that offenders spend incarcerated stunts any economic opportunity. White and middle-class individuals benefited from the decriminalization of the possession of small quantities of drugs; however, non-white individuals faced lengthier prison sentences (Roberts & Yu Chen, 2013).

Public opinion and reentry regulations regarding housing assistance are intersectional (Grommon, 2017). Many former inmates have difficulty finding employment to cover child support or housing. It is important to note how incarceration can increase the likelihood of relationship instability. Not to mention, ex-offenders may be returning to disadvantaged neighborhoods upon release from prison or jail, where they meet further strain. America's drug problem explains societal strain in urban areas. It is important to further examine such socioeconomic factors to understand why strains occur in impoverished communities, strains such as voter suppression, the lack of financial aid for higher education, and public housing. Grommon (2017) mentions the significance of collecting public opinion that translates transparency where the focus is on improving reentry by aiming at self-interest values held by the people.

Part Four:

Mass Incarceration as Social Control Formed by Public Opinion

America's rule-makers indirectly shape public opinion. Acts of racism that are publicized gives the okay to start an epidemic of strategic racism like the war on drugs caused. In reality, the relationship between public opinion and public policy is enigmatic and deeply complexed (Unnever & Cullen, 2010). The analogy of making America great again by building a wall to keep drugs outside of America creates a real moral panic concerning immigrants, regardless of status. By using the narrative of the war on drugs, previously honed by President Regan, symbolic rhetoric is utilized by America's leadership to place themselves as defenders of the vulnerable (youth) and the eradicator of law violators (drug offenders) (Yates & Whitford, 2009).

What can systematically control unfair sentencing disparities? Through the examination of political and popular rhetoric in America, society must emphasize how social control in the context of exploitation affects vulnerable populations. There exists a hyper-enforcement of policing that spearheads the assumption made by public fear and moral panic that immigrants, whether illegal or legal, are prone to crime. Therefore, social construction is built based on a false premise, which contributes to racial disparities, mainly through exclusion (Longazel, 2013).

Social control accounts for increased punitiveness of immigration and status. Race and racism are essential to comprehending why get-tough policies are supported by Americans (Unnever & Cullen, 2010). Disclosing how the product of privately operated immigration detention facilities set the tone for profitable industrial complexes is reproduced as a solution for direct control of vulnerable populations. Moreover, increased border control means that America will be detaining more illegals, thanks to a lucrative prison industry. As society lobbies for more punitive laws, criminalizing immigrants will increase and become more of a profitable solution (Longazel, 2013). Misleading the public to believe that drugs are an infinite problem entering the US borders is cause to link drug crimes and immigration subconsciously. The result of linking both crimes and immigration helps normalize private immigration detention centers, the disruption of families, and more extended stays for illegal immigrants behind bars. Longazel (2013) further ratiocinates how the US and Mexico border operated by more reinforcements than ever in the attempt to secure America's borders with walls, fences, cameras, patrols, and other security assets.

Social control theory can help explain the framework of how interactions with the law help shape legal socializations under social conditions. American citizens have some form of control on how laws are governed; furthermore, citizens have power if they can induce public officials to share a typical trajectory in their favor (Ingham, 2016). Ingham (2016) also posits that citizens have the power to confer rewards or penalties such as re-election or removal from office, which controls the behavior of these social agents. Even though citizens control the vote, citizens can also be strung along by unresearched rhetoric, which creates a biased agenda and further complicates racial disparities, primarily under federal sentencing guidelines.

The politics of criminalizing Latino immigrants is described in a way that allows the majority to steer away from strengthening much needed economic policies. Johnson et al. (2011) found that public opinion polls suggest the way White Americans perceive crime is associated with growing Latino populations, an important social problem in America. Therefore, the majority display a keen focus on immigrants and crime simultaneously (Longazel, 2013). By creating campaign advertisements and other propaganda, racial fear is produced without appearing overtly racist. Longazel (2013) further supports this racist list by providing an example of a racist ad President Bush's Willie Horton ad in 1988 that was not only explosive, but stoked racial fears. A form of presidential rhetoric that can be seen more currently, for example, is President Trump's controversial Luis Bracamontes ad in 2018 that showcases a fear of illegal immigrants and more crime.

Mass incarceration seems like a practical approach to appear anti-crime and to win the popular vote. However, the problem reflects the unsolved underlying cause for why people commit drug crimes, and it specifically targets the legal socialization of disadvantaged minority communities. Underprivileged minorities use the platform to solve crime by media reports and rhetoric from political hijackers. The political hijacker is an authority figure who pushes their own beliefs or agenda to enforce flawed policies based on empty rhetoric, not research.

Furthermore, mandatory minimum sentencing in a plethora of drug cases is subject to the influences of judicial and prosecutorial discretion. These minimums carry mandated sentences of 5 to 20 years, depending on the offense. Many claims have been made that America's criminal justice system is far from colorblind, reflecting that trial courts sentence Black Americans more rigidly than White Americans (Jacobs et al., 2007). The controversial mandatory minimums are the legal socialization of drug crimes because they are more severe, and there is a disparity of treatment between crack and powder cocaine as far as weight and sentencing calculations (Fischman & Schanzenbach, 2012).

Mass incarceration and public opinion are both interchangeable. Also, the establishment of support for alternative approaches to imprisonment such as rehabilitation is lacking, and calls to action that support of more punitive approaches to crime is a contributing factor. Different political framing makes various policies more or less likely in which proper representation in criminal justice reform matters. Political framing relates to creating one's narrative about an issue (usually dealing with race and crime) with relatively little to no objective or impartial insight. Furthermore, when Black Americans highly represent the number of those incarcerated, White Americans are less likely to support petitions for prison reform, including three-strike laws and stop and frisk policies (Drakulich & Kirk, 2016).

The problem is the lack of reframing that occurs in the role of criminal justice reform. If the etiology of mass incarceration, mandatory minimum sentencing, stop and frisk, and unjust prison sentences are not well researched or publicly acknowledged, no one will understand its consequences. Disparities in sentencing policies will be less prevalent in criminal justice reform by the public. For public opinion to effectively influence social control, the exposure of the failures of the current criminal justice system must be exposed, further analyzed, and made clear to the public.

Part Five:
Black and Latino Voting in Local Elections

Here it is argued that social control theory influences public opinion by way of voting in local elections. Black Americans and Latinos must know the significance and impacts of voting in local elections. Potential presidential candidates are often those Senators and Mayors who once were responsible for disparities such as stop and frisk and the mass incarceration of Black and Latino citizens. Prison reform to include racial disparities in prison sentences is very important and plays a role in voting. Jacobs et al. (2007) suggest the size of the minority vote needed simply to reach the point where the minority vote help sways an election.

It is no secret that America's politicians encourage individuals to vote based on their views about the death penalty. After all, criminal justice is inseparably political. Furthermore, many believe that the death penalty replaces socialized and legalized codes enforced through Jim Crow. It is significant to examine Jim Crow with current criminal justice policies because these historical events affect current legal decisions about who should live and who should die (Jacobs et al., 2005). Furthermore, Gross, Possley & Stephens (2017) proclaim that innocent Black Americans are 3.5 times more likely than innocent White Americans to be convicted of sexual assault, 7 times more likely to be convicted of murder, and 12 times more likely to be convicted of drug crimes.

The former Mayor of New York City, Michael Bloomberg, pushed stop-and-frisk policies for the city of New York during his term as Mayor. He is the same former Mayor who was a presidential candidate for 2020, now apologetic about a policy that screamed institutionalized racism. Black Americans and Latinos alike have the opportunity to vote against racist policies leaving them to rot behind prison walls or face police intimidation and harassment. It is well-documented through research that such racial disparities are alive and well, resulting from both policing by policy and by practice. Heightened alertness and police emphasis shines a spotlight on certain groups of people. Because of specific policing policies such as stop-and-frisk, law enforcement targets racial minorities. Moreover, law enforcement practices of issuing warnings versus actual arrests for certain groups of people in comparison to others results in racial disparities, especially amongst male Black and Latino youth 18 years of age and younger (Kahn & Martin, 2016).

Many Black and Latino people believe their voice is silenced; therefore, their vote does not count. However, criminal justice reform is local. Imagine not having a voice heard in policies that have gotten away with institutionalized racism. It is well-researched that citizens who are threatened by the increase of Black American and Latino presence, counter their perceived threat by demanding harsh criminal justice policies. Furthermore, since criminal justice agencies are state-operated, the push has to be directed at political representatives (Jacob et al., 2007).

The anticipated outcome of this section is to embark on a tragedy involving a woman of color facing police brutality in an era that only highlighted police brutality of Black males. Black American males that are harassed by law enforcement officers are more likely to be represented in media reports. Black America could no longer brace for the blatant racial impact of women being added to the issue of police brutality. To shed a bright light on racial discrimination within the criminal justice system against women is the trajectory. It is not rocket science to figure out if racial discrimination exists in the criminal justice system. To further examine this racial discrimination, one must uncover the racial history of the criminal justice system. While peeling back layers of the onion, one will truly discover how the Jim Crow era is the core that hardensthe old practice of behavior-modifying, and how this practice has evolved into present-day. Jim Crow laws enforced racial tension in America, and its insidious history has toxified the current criminal justice system against minorities.

Black Americans have made significant strides in recent political opportunities. As an increased number of Black Americans win municipal and national political offices, racial tensions and racial competition can alter (Parker, Stults & Rice, 2005). While there are some improvements implemented within the criminal justice system, one will delineate and hopefully ratiocinate examples of past events to shed light on current events that contribute to racial discrimination in America. To understand the next level of how criminal justice disparities impacts race relations, one must examine history, and eliminate egregious errors within the system starting with law enforcement officers.

Part Six:
Remember Her Name

In 2015, a young, Black, and pulchritudinous woman was pulled over during a traffic stop violation for failing to signal ended in tragedy. The situation escalated abruptly and ended tragically. The woman allegedly assaulted the law enforcement officer during a routine traffic stop. Thanks to technology and social media, the capture of excessive force (from an eyewitness' cellular phone), confirmed what may have been officer misconduct. After her violent arrest, the young woman's lifeless body was found hanging in her cell.

This case reflects the enforcement of the Jim Crow era when Black and White Americans faced different rules to abide by. Black Americans are insidiously targeted for modern day lynching. Communities will never forget her Sandra Bland, a name that sparked national controversy amongst the Black community and law enforcement. Although the Civil Rights Act of 1964 dismantled segregation laws known as Jim Crow, racial discrimination still exists within the criminal justice system.

In order to grasp the concept of racial discrimination in the criminal justice system, one should examine the history of the Jim Crow era. These were laws that kept Black Americans oppressed, especially in the justice system. In the time of Jim Crow, there was much documentation of Black American riders involved in physical altercations, their ejections from buses, and their arrests by local law enforcement. Because of the continuous injustice that Black Americans faced, weariness grew amongst them, a fatigue which prompted Rosa Parks to refuse to give up her seat to a White passenger in 1955.

Police officers, judges, and other authoritative law enforcement professionals also wore white hoods and terrorized Black American communities. The act of war on Black communities is a prime example of the history of institutionalized racism that is still relevant today that is witnessed in courtrooms and behind prison walls. Banks (2017) suggests that Black Americans have suffered discrimination initially throughout the system of slavery, then through exclusion and segregation with Jim Crow in the shape of legislation and court decisions that have historically endorsed overt racial discrimination. Before the death of Bland, she was charged with a possession of a small amount of marijuana. Furthermore, one in five people Bland's age were smoking marijuana that year nationally; however, minorities were more likely to be criminally charged (Nathan, 2016). Unfortunately, occurrences of an unjust criminal justice system such as this are another form of modern-day lynching of people of color (Unever & Cullen, 2010).

Racial profiling is a common form of racial discrimination today that people of color often face. Wilson, Wilson, & Thou (2015) delineates how racial profiling has become systematically institutionalized as a part of law enforcement culture. This practice must be eradicated from the ground-up immediately, that police appear to disproportionately arrest or ticket persons of color. Thus, Black Americans have been stereotyped by police officers as criminals (Wilson et al., 2015).

Now that the establishment of racial discrimination exist within the criminal justice system, discovering ways to mitigate racial hate is important. One of the ways is through community policing efforts. Police officers are allowed to enter Black American neighborhoods when they encounter drugs or violence. Community members often express minimal trust for law enforcement officers in some neighborhoods.

In places such as St. Louis, when the police kill someone of color, it's very aggressive at the scene and a lot of people do not shy from the fact that it's aggressive. If a law enforcement officer comes into one of these Black communities, and draw their weapon, it is highly likely that these law enforcement officers are met with resistance (Green et al., 2016). On the other hand, it is enigmatic how Banks (2017) suggests that there are other communities that generally deny that racial discrimination occurs in their neighborhoods. These individuals lack the fear of being a victim to violent crime. However, these community members are afraid about potential racial discrimination in law enforcement occurring beyond their communities.

Community policing has been increasingly promoted in other parts of the world outside of the United States. In Asia, to reduce the fear of crime within communities as well as to overcome mutual distrust amongst law enforcement and community members, police-citizen partnerships through short-term workshops are promoted (Kocak, 2018). Cooperation effort is productive. In America, individuals do not view racial disparities within the criminal justice system as a matter of greater importance; however, they believe that it does exist and disapprove of the behavior (Banks, 2017).

When police officers get involved in the communities they serve in an ethical manner, mistrust and racial discrimination becomes an irrelevant issue. Community policing challenges crime, and more importantly, it mitigates fear. It involves dedication and effort amongst both parties. So, when events occur like Sandra Bland's case, one will only pray that racial discrimination is dismantled accordingly. The issue is there is no definitive accountability. Due to racial discrimination, such as racial profiling, many Black American men and women are now hashtags. The Black American community remembers the names of the unarmed victims so that community members can fight for social justice and end racial discrimination. The first step is to acknowledge that Jim Crow style policing still lingers within the ranks of law enforcement from the top-down. Communities must unite and confront faulty law enforcement using education and social platforms to implement better policies and good police tactics.

What happened to Sandra Bland in 2015 was a tragedy; no one was held accountable. Therefore, society should learn from that case, as well as the countless other cases involving police brutality targeted at Black Americans. Rickford (2016) explained how the organization of the Black community through vigils and rallies in support of murdered Black women have directly contributed to the stories pertaining to Black women who have faced alarming rates of police assault and incarceration. Outreach is how society remember their names.

Many offenders are awaiting death row after facing capital charges. It is in the following section that the death penalty is reevaluated for offenders where there is evidence that may exonerate them from their crimes.

Part Seven:
When the Justice System Fails Black Americans

When the justice system fails Black Americans, it is not only enigmatic but unfortunate. It could lead to tragedies experienced by the family and the entire community. Sometimes these tragedies create national outrage, especially when stemming from systematic racism. Here, I would like to examine the role of death row and how it impacts Black Americans serving life behind bars facing death. The assumption can be made that if a Black person kills a law enforcement officer, they will be automatically sentenced to death. However, when law enforcement officers shoot and kill unarmed Black Americans, the officers are sent home with paid, administrative leave. Very rarely are officers held accountable for the lives of Black unarmed civilians.

On March 5, 2020, *CNN* reports that the state of Alabama executes Nathaniel Woods, who was convicted of capital murder as an accomplice. Linked to the killings of three Birmingham officers in 2004, Mr. Woods met his demise. The officers were pursuing a drug house, where Mr. Woods was placed with his assailant, Kerry Spencer, who is also on death row. Mr. Spencer wrote a letter confessing that he acted alone when he shot and killed the three officers. He also alleged that Mr. Woods ran when he heard the shots being fired (McLaughlin, Savidge & Sanchez, 2020).

The execution of Nathaniel Woods was a tragedy because, although a jury sentenced him to death, executions are not carried out until, on average, fifteen years later (Gershowitz, 2016). Mr. Woods may not have pulled the trigger to kill the three officers; however, some felt that Mr. Woods was an engaged participant and hardly a bystander. A plethora of pleads set out on Mr. Wood's behalf, to include celebrities, still did not stop his untimely execution.

Presidents and governors can attach conditions to commutations (Gershowitz, 2016). However, Governor of Alabama, Kay Ivey, allowed the execution to proceed as scheduled. Mr. Wood's execution was seen by many as an act of revenge for three police officers being killed. Gershowitz (2016) suggests that mercy and rehabilitation take a backseat to retribution and deterrence. Unsurprisingly, governors become less willing to grant clemency.

According to the Death Penalty Information Center (2020), in the state of Virginia, twenty-one prosecutors signed a letter to repeal capital punishment. Virginia's jurors have not imposed a death sentence in over eight years. The high cost of death-penalty cases, the arbitrary application of death sentences, the risk of wrongful convictions, and the lack of deterrent effect are reasons for the revocation of capital punishment.

Enforcing life imprisonment or execution for killing police officers is another strategic tactic to cease moral panic. When law enforcement officers take the lives of unarmed Americans, the punishment is not as extreme for them. It instead suggests that the officer's judgment was justified because their lives were potentially placed in danger. Imagine when citizens feel that their lives are in danger by the people that were sworn to protect them? Are there any harsh penalties for those who bring disservice to the honor of wearing a badge? The punishment should fit the crime on both sides of the fence: law enforcement officers and citizens.

Spending life behind bars or being sentenced to execution is a definitive matter. Because our judicial system is not error-free, assiduous investigation and thorough research regarding the case should be examined without prejudice. Innocent women and men who have been wrongly convicted of crimes and sentenced to death are exonerated. If the ex-offenders lacked mental health issues before, they probably have them now! Imagine the trauma, the lingering effects of being confined, and the emotional and psychological stress that occurs. So, what is the impact of surviving the death penalty? Westervelt & Cook (2018) conducted research on the aftermath of being exonerated from death row. The duo has found fewer death row occupants are released because of evidence of their factual innocence, and grueling years of legal challenges are the reality for those who are released ascertaining their renewed freedom.

Part Eight:
The School to Prison Pipeline

This section will analyze minority juveniles and law enforcement contact, and the lack of training thereof. Referring to specific training that can be beneficial to authorities when encountering disadvantaged youth in an educational setting is essential. The assumption can be made that minority youth are exposed to environments where their behaviors in school are criminalized, rather than assiduously addressed with behavioral health and community support. They are given one leg up in the battle of unjust sentencing early on in life. The increased presence in America's schools result in approximately 10,000 charges for disorderly conduct each school year (Bleakley & Bleakley, 2018).

Black American and Latino youth are introduced to the criminal justice system early on. The school-to-prison pipeline is problematic because the results from placing law enforcement officers in schools influence student accomplishments, attitudes, and behaviors. The way that schools discipline youth with prison-like environments is more insidious to student's wellbeing than schools with fewer discipline policies (Mallett, 2017). Additionally, the school-to-prison pipeline contributes to unfair sentencing because it targets students of color and criminalizes education. Urban communities believe that their children's safety and protection are priority. However, the reality reflects the pretenses of limited choices in a direction headed straight from school into America's incarceration system. Mallet (2017) emphasizes maltreatment as a cogent agent for many youths, and is linked to school discipline because of trauma-related problems.

The zero-tolerance attitude used to deter minor offenses contributes to limited learning opportunities. Unfortunately, minorities must seek a level playing field to compete with their white counterparts. Any hope of a future filled with inclusion is decrepitated when school resource officers, metal detectors, extra security cameras, and security guards are prevalent in urban American schools. With a philosophy that screams zero tolerance, any minor misconduct insidiously impacts the future of these kids and the contact they face with law enforcement into adulthood (Bleakley & Bleakley, 2018).

The school-to-prison pipeline must be dismantled by effective evidence-based practices that actually works. Also, any changes to school safety policies to bring sanguine reinforcement in schools (behavioral health services to include counseling, mentorship programs, before-and-after school programs, community involvement, training programs for SROs) will serve as a crucial gain in the needs of students.

In this section, the delineation of specific solutions is analyzed to solving the pipeline crisis in urban America's school systems. Assiduous attention to factors contributing to more law enforcement contact inside of schools explains inconsistencies. Moreover, mental health training is a valuable tool amongst uniformed officers if done strategically and adequately for the protection of officers, juveniles, and the community.

Punishments employed by authorities often have insidious effects as they cause strain, isolation from society, and foster the social learning of crime (Agnew & Brezina, 2015). It is important to establish training that aides in correcting delinquent behavior that mitigates these harmful effects. There is some training for law enforcement officers that engage in a way that rebuilds the ties between offenders and the community by addressing mental health and ways to engage it efficiently while protecting the community from dangerous offenders. The detailed description of a specific training program for uniformed officers targeting mental health juveniles will highlight strategic ways of reducing delinquency. Specific training programs that targets the development of the juvenile's brain, recognize differences between youth and adults, and approach mental health without disrupting community-based sanctions are needed.

Part Nine:
Juveniles, the Brain and Neuroscience

Research highlights the significance of adolescent youth being seen in a period of developmental vulnerabilities. To further explain, the part of the brain that is significant in learning to include storing memory is the hippocampus, and it continues to develop into adolescence. The pre-frontal cortex is another portion of the brain that involves the regulation of emotional behaviors, executive function, and fear. Like the hippocampus, the PFC continues to mature in juveniles. Lastly, the amygdala plays a significant role in emotional memory and fear conditioning (Romero & McEwen, 2006).

Additionally, changes in a youth's nervous system, physiology, and behavior are orchestrated by puberty. This cognitive information is relevant to mental health training because School Resource Officers (SROs) encounter juveniles who are experiencing puberty, on top of struggling with mental health issues inside the academic environment. It also provides insight for SROs to understand how juvenile and adult brain development differentiate when considering stress (Romero & McEwen, 2006). With learning how the cognitive mind differs for juveniles, it would be enigmatic to subject these youth to unjust sentencing and mass incarceration.

Law enforcement officers could benefit from training when encountering juveniles who present mental health challenges. *Miller v. Alabama* and *Jackson v. Hobbs* are both cases that prove why law enforcement officers must be better aware of the various cognitive differences in youth and adults. Moreover, juveniles have more unsatisfactory judgment than adults (Cohen & Casey, 2014). Therefore, juveniles must not be treated in the same manner as adults, nor should they be exposed to the same punishments.

SROs are uniformed police officers. The trajectory of their work is to make schools safer by preventing crime. They can also respond to escalated situations that become problematic in schools as they are a bridge between the community and the educator for the advocacy of students. These uniform officers partake in required specialty training when working with youth. These specific roles SRO play within the school system differs across states, as well as state legislation delineating grant programs for developing training (Pentek & Eisenberg, 2018).

Mental Health training can assist SROs by equipping them with the tools necessary to build better communities as well as relationships with law enforcement officers. Fry, O'Riordan & Geanellos (2002) showed how policing individuals with mental health issues incorporate uniformed officers in a mental health team. Including these officers as active participants in mental health programs helps SROs properly combat delinquency and mental health.

Mental health training provides SROs with resources to use when coming up with a plan to assist the youth by providing an alternative to incarceration. SROs can also learn insights to understanding the needs of youth. SROs can learn to empathize with youth because they are not exempt from mental health issues themselves (COPS, 2016). SROs can get mental health training from the National Association of School Resource Officers (NASRO). NASRO is a non-profit membership organization made up of school-based law enforcement officers, school administrators, and school security officers (Counts et al., 2018). This organization provides training to school-based law enforcement officers as well as educators called Adolescent Mental Health Training for School Resource Officers and Educators (AMHT).

Adolescent Mental Health Training for School Resource Officers and Educators (AMHT) is a school resource officer training that aids SROs with the ability to identify and respond to youth who need mental health services. The trajectory of training is to develop the critical skills and the ability to respond to behavior issues that can be seen in youth with mental health issues (NASRO, 2014). The training provides a framework for how SROs respond and interact to juveniles. To further explain why this training is needed, students with disabilities represent only 12% of the total population; however, students with disabilities account for 28% of all arrests and referrals (Counts et al., 2018). The ideal thing about AMHT is that it is a team approach to tackling mental health issues within the school environment.

The AMHT curriculum is based on the SRO's ability to understand youth development; understand youth mental health conditions, learn and practice crisis intervention, de-escalate procedures, communicate with juveniles, discuss roles they play in the schools, learn about the significance of family roles, and learn what service options for services are available to help juveniles. Furthermore, it helps the trainee understand what healthy youth development is and the impact of environmental factors on the development of the brain's psychosocial development. Psychosocial development is achieved by examining the brain and its different stages of the development, which affects emotions, cognitive processes, and social functioning, i.e. how youth make decisions and behave. The AMHT training specifically ratiocinates many common mental health problems that youth face and how to introduce comprehensive treatment for these mental health issues. They also learn about suicide factors, risks, and potential for self-harm in juveniles. Moreover, the training allows for SROs to identify skills to adequately engage with students experiencing these issues while still embracing school policy (NASRO, 2014).

Research suggests that the implementation of many SRO programs is due to the response to school violence and the allocated funding available. Furthermore, a specialized curriculum for SROs should include juvenile justice code and legal issues, child development, communication techniques, and specialized populations, including minorities and students with disabilities (Counts et al., 2018).

Respect is a core value that goes a long way when addressing the needs of juveniles with mental health challenges. Attentiveness and consideration are both types of respect needed to prepare training programs for law enforcement and leaders to engage with youth. Strategies must be applied for support, and it takes a village. When using respect, it allows community leaders to come together harmoniously. Agnew & Brezina (2015) suggests that training programs employ strategy. First, community leaders must be made aware of such training programs in order to enlist support. Community leaders are people like the mayor, police chief, judges, school superintendent, businesses, civic and religious communities, as well as representatives from state and federal agencies. Second, when rendering support, this pool of people take responsibility for spearheading and implementing training programs. Lastly, after these teams of people receive the training themselves, they can identify community problems that spark juvenile delinquency, and they examine resources that are utilized to handle such problems in the community. Also, this group of people takes the initiative to design an approach for engaging community problems identified through training.

SROs can benefit a lot from mental health training for juveniles through attending AMHT services. Through the training process, SROs can develop empathy and ways to engage youth in a respectful, humane, and effective way in order to contribute to identifying community problems through training. If the trajectory of SROs in school is to make school environments safer, than programs such as AMHT become ideal because they address ways to model implementation on prevention and rehabilitation of at-risk juvenile delinquents in school settings. In order for AMHT to be a success, SROs must understand the cognitive development of juveniles and practice de-escalation methods, crisis management, and various mental health issues plaguing youth. The time of adolescence is a period of developmental vulnerabilities considering parts of the brain are still developing well into adolescence.

Part Ten:
Disproportionate Minority Contact Policy

Young, Black Americans are largely represented in the criminal justice system. Therefore, these youth make up the demographics of overrepresentation throughout the range of juvenile justice, constituting a whopping 16 percent in the US; however, they make-up 31 percent of all referrals to court, 35 percent petitions, 33 percent determined delinquent, and lastly, 52 percent committed to secure facilities (Donnelly, 2017). Alarming results as such is the bases for progression to be made toward minority involvement in the justice system.

Both education and absent parenting are factors of delinquency and juvenile's encountering the justice system. Juvenile probation officers can rectify these factors by creating structured, content-specific methods to referral processes as well as targeting the deinstitutionalization of offenders. Research of all prevention and rehabilitation programs, must focus on factors that cause delinquency.

The DMC is a symbol of a policy enforcing state juvenile justice officials to do something about racial disparities within the justice system. Congress created the DMC to mitigate the increased minority encounters in secure facilities. However, this provision blasted federally funded states to decrease the number of minority groups that were detained and confined if the percentages exceeded the numbers of the group in relation to the general public. But some believed that this policy would cease the tainted justice system in allowing white privilege to have advantages of restorative sanctions and giving minorities the disadvantage of confinement into secure facilities. In response, Congress revised the DMC in order to provide a more effective response to racial disparities.

This meant that there must be a specific change to juvenile processing while strengthening juvenile delinquency prevention efforts. A rework of the DMC would suggest to the policymakers that states would be inspired to invest in before-and-after school programs, treatment and diversion programs set-up to assist youth who are at-risk before they encounter sanctions of delinquency and confinement. Congress tried to be proactive with the revision. The reformulated approach to the DMC in 2002 was met with a federally funded state to mitigate the disproportionate number of minorities facing the juvenile justice system without the use of quota standards (Donnelly, 2017).

Unsupervised youth can become problematic in terms of juvenile delinquency. Outside of the juvenile justice system, unsupervised youth unfortunately impact the high level of DMC. Overall, mothers and fathers are both significantly important when rearing children; however, focus on absent fathers in minority communities is noteworthy for research and further discussion. Research posits that disadvantaged youth are more likely to grow up in fatherless homes due to marital rates being low and fertility rates amongst disadvantage populations being high. Therefore, incarceration and the absence of fathers in disadvantage households present socioeconomic antecedents, which becomes fuel for establishing a delinquent pattern. This population is also at a disservice, resulting in hardship, such as poverty and racial inequalities. Specifically, father absence increases the chances of incarceration for male youth (Harper, 2004).

It is important to consider the significance of a sanguine and cogent male role-model present in disadvantaged households to prevent DMC. As both community leaders and policymakers recognize a father's potential to decrease youth involvement with the justice system, further research posits that the quality of a father and child relationship is predictive of delinquent behavior and substance use that is greater and beyond maternal involvement (Simmons et al., 2018).

Another factor outside of the justice system that impacts the high level of DMC is the lack of education in at-risk communities. In many communities school is a safe haven for most youth. However, as a response to deviant behavior, schools commonly use punitive consequences that place youth outside of the learning environment and school activities where they can thrive. Because of this, the removal of youth from the school environment is not effective in the mitigation of problem behavior and academic progression. In fact, removal from school to include suspensions and expulsions actually increases as a sanction in middle school. As a result, expanding upon a more punitive disciplinary action in schools, the process often exacerbates emotional as well as behavioral problems (Rusby et al., 2011).

Juvenile probation officers can potentially reduce DMC by deinstitutionalizing juvenile status offenders. When emphasizing the deinstitutionalization of juveniles, it is important to delineate the procedures for mitigating incarcerated youth. In greater detail, reference can be made to increase the removal of youth from secure detention, the increased removal of youth from secure institutions, and the increased prevention of youth from out of home placement which would have been otherwise placed in secure confinement (Mahoney, 1981). Juvenile probation officers can assist by embarking on the impact of juvenile treatment, family dynamics, and deciphering the negative effects that may imbalance the positive to reduce recidivism rates. Juvenile probation officers can recommend that juvenile delinquents who have not committed serious crimes receive community-based services, extensive counseling, and alternative education where there is thorough follow-up upon completion.

Another way that juvenile probation officers can potentially reduce DMC is by way of program referral. Juvenile probation officers have a referral process after a juvenile is booked or cited. The referral process is intervention that usually takes place at the disposition phase. There are often partnerships that take place amongst the juvenile justice system and community-based programs designed for intervention. These programs have the trajectory to reduce recidivism with hopes of facilitating better outcomes for juvenile delinquents. More significantly, juvenile probation officers can investigate the mechanism by which juveniles are referred. This process must be done to ensure that the proper programming is being issued to the right youth for the appropriate reasons, whether an option is given based on biased tendencies (Campbell et al., 2018).

The core value of respect applies to the brief history of prevention and rehabilitation regarding juveniles. Agnew & Brezina (2015) suggest that rehabilitation fell out of favor in the past history by the reinforcement of studies in the 1970s and 1980s that suggested it was ineffective. However, in the past few years, there has been a renewed interest in prevention and rehabilitation regarding respect for punishment, prevention, and rehabilitation. All three approaches can be equally effective in deterring juvenile delinquency as long as the proper respect and detail to thorough research made readily available to show public interest in prevention and rehabilitative programs. For juveniles who are not deemed dangerous, other methods seem more plausible.

Each state should take the time to treat and rehabilitate youth, and not harden them through severe punishment. The review of prevention and rehabilitation programs is the way to measure the effectiveness of mitigating delinquency. Unfortunately, many individuals and groups are unaware of this information to control delinquency in juveniles. By becoming keen on reviews of research as a society, everyone can tentatively and respectively state the most effective prevention and rehabilitation programs by focusing on the major causes of delinquency, in which many efforts have no clear focus (Agnew & Brezina, 2015).

Young minority juveniles are largely represented in the juvenile justice system. Often, they are disproportionately impacted by bias decision-making processes by the justice system. However, outside of the juvenile justice system, factors that impact high levels of DMC are parental absence as well as education. If parents, specifically the presence of a cogent black father, is not present in the lives of at-risk youth, these youth become vulnerable to the juvenile justice system.

Difficulty in school often arises by the time of middle school. In this population, students may face sanctions of expulsion or suspension from school. If education is a factor that can aid youth from further becoming a statistic of DMC, then it serves a better purpose for at-risk students to be in a school where they can continue to learn. This section also addressed both ways that juvenile probation officers can contribute to the reduction of DMC, and that is by revisiting their referral process, as well as advocating for the deinstitutionalization of juvenile offenders. Future research is needed to determine the characteristics of successful prevention as well as rehabilitation efforts. There is a strong need to promote respect for research in order to gain insight on the appropriate action supporting juvenile recidivism.

Imagine living in a society where paranoia sets in on the regular because of the crimes committed by juveniles. Influential criminologists who fueled publicized crimes committed by juveniles with theoretical analysis of a predatorial myth has changed the way juveniles are brought to justice and institutionalized. The trajectory of ending DMC delineates how public fear gathered from limited research and data results in harsher punishments for juveniles. This fear will disproportionately affect a specific group of juveniles over another, instead of examining other ways to answer the call of public demands in deterring juvenile violence.

Part Eleven:
The Super Predator

A social scientist by the name of Dr. John Dilulio coined the term "super predator". Dr. Dilulio possessed an extreme outlook regarding youth violence. He proclaimed that the United States is a demographic time bomb that will explode. Dr. Dilulio posited that juvenile males will increase by 500,000, and many of these kids will be raised in moral poverty. They will be raised in the midst of deviant, delinquent, and criminal adults who partake in abusive, violence, fatherless, Godless, and jobless circumstances. Because of this rough history Black's faced, these "super predators" will unleash a new era of deviance (Stanley, 2015). Dr. Dilulio had a strong outlook on juveniles of the inner-city. His solution for the Black American community was the inner-city church. Dr. Dilulio (1996) testifies regarding Black delinquents, suggesting jails and churches are the best solutions to counter-violence as a dangerous social trend.

In the late 1990s, policymakers responded to public pressure formed by highly publicized crime in the juvenile population by tightening existing laws on repeat offenders (Kovandzic, Sloan & Vieraitis, 2002). Not only did this action inflict lengthier prison sentences on these juveniles, it also disproportionately impacted juveniles of color. Voisin, et al. (2017) posits Black American youth, in comparison with other peer ethnic groups, overrepresent the population in the American juvenile justice system. Perhaps there are social, political, and economic factors that contribute to juvenile crime. The problem is the egregious process in which the law is used to deter crime.

Furthermore, catering to the super predator concept, the solution to deter crime amongst a fragile population is to condemn them with extreme sentencing while institutionalizing them to become monsters. These juveniles have little to no contact with family and not to mention any educational trajectory becomes less of a priority behind prison walls. Inmates who are sentenced as juveniles and are now adults coming out of prison have criminal records and limited job skills, they're released into society like a stranger moving into foreign territory.

The impact that law enforcement has on the super predator myth is the tactics used to profile juveniles who fit the description of monsters. Research has unveiled explicit and implicit discriminatory practices and insidious stereotypes that are influenced by the experiences and treatment of minority juveniles. There is also differential treatment in practices used by law enforcement, especially regarding the zero-tolerance school policies in inner-city communities. These efforts increase the chances of minority juvenile's affiliation with the juvenile justice system early on from school-to-prison (Campbell et al., 2018). It is through the experience that some minorities have with officers that lead them to the belief that law enforcement canvas specific areas, looking for a super predator. An example being, the police officer shooting 12-year-old Tamir Rice, who was holding a toy gun in 2014.

The impact corrections have on the super predatory myth is the theoretical basis used in the risk assessment and risk assessment instruments utilized to identify risks for recidivism. Risk assessments such as the risk–need–responsivity (RNR) model helps identify attitudes and behaviors of individual juveniles as well as the micro-level criminogenic risk factors that impacts a juvenile's risk of reoffending. Although the risk assessments are utilized to promote equal treatment, how the collection of the information on these risk assessments are linked with specific subgroups, can leave room for bias and discrimination (Campbell et al., 2018).

The impact of the super predator myth within the courts occurs when poorly performed risk assessments are handled for certain groups of juveniles. Examining court practices and procedures may be worth further research and investigation to explore recidivism in juvenile courts by race, gender, and social class. The negative perceptions and stereotypes about minority juveniles suggest that they need the most help, they are a threat to society, which impacts them disproportionality in court (Campbell et al., 2018). There is always public pressure for the courts to be tough on crime due to public fear and moral panic. However, according to The Office of Juvenile Justice and Delinquency Prevention (OJJDP) (2018), the arrest rate for juveniles ages ten to 17 years of age across all offenses peaked in 1996 before it declined by 72 percent in 2017.

Expounding upon the life-altering experiences from the Exonerated Five, the term super predator was used to dehumanize and demonize them. They were teenagers who also served lengthy prison sentences for a crime that DNA evidence exonerated them from later as adults. When terms like super predator are given cogency, the meaning can be weaponized. And in the case of the Exonerated Five, criminalized. The value of respect must be reflected in media coverage, the justice system, as well as society. It is important that stakeholders respect all aspects of the judicial process in order for it to be effective.

The social construction perspective provides a ratiocination of understanding how the presence of mass media influences society's perceptions. The social construction perspective enables the sense of public influence on perceptions of crime and justice-related issues. The topic of juvenile drug possession and abuse will impact the attitudes society has about accountability, and about the individuals who commit these acts. Sometimes, the media's inaccurate depiction of crime and the criminal justice system is what fuels people's perceptions about the nature of crime and how the justice system should work (Rhineberger-Dunn, Briggs & Rader, 2016).

As a definitive reflection of this section, the super predator myth caused more harm than good in many communities. Unfortunately, there are still individuals behind bars due to crimes committed as juveniles. The negative impact of justice is that justice does not always come blind. When a specific group of people are labeled with derogatory terms, they are dehumanized as aliens, monsters, and even super predators. Society views the dehumanized as less than, not worthy, and they become more vulnerable. Not only is the dehumanization of racial and ethnic groups based upon flawed logic, it is also a non-sequitur in that the data and research do not support the harshness of tough on crime laws.

Part Twelve:
Reliability of an Accusatory Process:
False Confessions

In this section, it is important to touch on the methods in which people of color are interviewed and interrogated. What makes people who are innocent, confess to crimes they have not committed? The trajectory of relaying such information is to critically analyze the Reid interviewing method's inability to conform reliability within its efforts of confession. The Reid process is a familiar type of interviewing technique that investigators go to when questioning suspects. As it appears to be the gold standard in interrogation efforts, the light shines on a plethora of reasons why it is not for juveniles as well as individuals with mental disabilities or illnesses.

Additionally, the Reid technique may not be the appropriate method of interrogating all suspects to include juveniles and people who have learning disabilities or do not possess the knowledge of basic legal rights, as this technique is very accusatory and could be a dangerous tool to use with the wrong population. After the discovery of the Central Park Jogger Case of 1989, the accused were sentenced to prison for an act they were coaxed into admitting to guilt, despite their innocence. Pearse (1995) posits an interesting cognitive struggle develops when law enforcement is presented with information or discovering through facts that challenge their preconceptions through interviewing.

The Exonerated Five were boys at the time of the Central Park jogger crime. DNA evidence eventually exonerated them, but one should not forget the hours and hours of interrogation, which resulted in them confessing that they were guilty of a crime. Although not illegal, the Reid technique presents ethical concerns for minors and people with mental disabilities. It is important for law enforcement officers who use this technique to ensure that suspects are treated well, that they are not threatened, that no promises are made, and that the suspect's confession is not forced. Minors and individuals with a mental disability should know that they have legal rights before being interviewed.

The confrontational style method of interviewing using the Reid technique is not only controversial but demeaning for individuals whose brains are not equipped to function like a "normal" adult. The total brain size is approximately 90 percent of its adult size by the age of 6; however, the gray and white matter subcomponents of the brain undergo dynamic changes throughout adolescence. (Casey, Jones & Somerville, 2011).

Vrij (2008) posits that when a young child and an adult both lie about the same occurrence, can both lies be distinguished. As most individuals would probably suggest, the young child's mendacity is more accessible to distinguish. However, they do not have the cognitive abilities to make up plausible lies, realize that making a credible impression is significant, or possess the muscular control needed to display an honest demeanor. It is enigmatic how youth can be subject to the Reid technique similar to adults. The Reid technique has the trajectory of making a suspect uncomfortable while they acknowledge whatever truthfulness is there.

In applying the Reid technique, the investigator psychologically ascertains information pertaining to the case by establishing a good rapport with the suspect in a monologue style. However, the technique may certainly be misapplied by some law enforcement officers. Some law enforcement officers would use the technique even when they are unsure of the accused's guilt. They also provide the interviewee or suspect with any evidence ascertained against them. The evidence may be mendacities or the truth. It is more of a psychological dramaturgy as the scene set up for the suspect is well planned from the style of the room to the type of chair the suspect is seated in.

Furthermore, the investigator attempts to persuade the interviewee that they committed the crime or were involved. This approach is supposed to make the interviewee nervous. The investigator typically invades personal space and make the interviewee uncomfortable in a subtle way. Imagine being a child. Imagine being mentally disabled. Imagine being powerless. Investigators generally use the same interrogation measures with juveniles and adults, which makes any confession coercive. In a Reid training event that entailed an instructional amount of training, "only 10 minutes of instruction was dedicated to youth and this was to advocate the use of the same strategies with youth as with adults" (Meyer & Reppucci, 2007). This type of method of strategy utilized can present an overwhelming occurrence of errors.

The case, *R. v. Thaher, 2016 ONCJ 113* focused on the refusal to admit a Reid-based interview-style confession by a mentally ill man who was fatigued, accused of attempted murder, and interrogated for more than seven hours. It is an oppressive measure used by interrogators and can be the cause of false confessions. The elements of the technique used were minimizing the offense when communicating with the suspect, the refusal of proclaims of innocence from the suspect, extreme time used for questioning designed to deflect the suspect's innocence, and providing the suspect with false evidence. While it is legal for interrogators to present evidence they have not actually ascertained, there are visible dangers. Presenting a suspect with fabricated evidence has the potential to persuade the suspect of admitting guilt, or at least to convince the suspect that any profession of innocence is worthless.

Interviewing techniques and tactical reliability observation help paint a picture of observation as a useful tool in the reliability process. It is also considered a valid method of assessing reliability through observation. In order for this process to be effective, the observer should be trained and unbiased. They must know how to separate observation from interpretation, as it inclines the reliability of the observation. Lastly, learning to observe body language, facial expressions, as well as listening to vocal nuances, can reflect more about personality without using words (Vrij, 2008).

There is a stereotypical view that liars have a behavior of acting more nervously than honest people, which could undoubtedly arise from the act of accusing someone of lying. For example, when a suspect is sweating during an interview or stumble over their words. Moreover, to defuse the suspect in believing that they are innocent, the investigator may accuse the suspect of being deceitful. Accusations could result in the suspect displaying symptoms of nervousness such as increased movement, but this can occur in both innocent and guilty suspects. Unbeknownst to the investigator, their accusations may guide them to believe that nervous behavior is equivalent to being untruthful (Vrij, 2008).

There is a plethora of fundamental inconsistencies regarding the integrity of law enforcement interviews, which not only includes reliability and the admissibility of such confessions, but of the confidence, the public has in the criminal justice system (Pearse, 1995). The Reid technique may not be the gold standard of interrogation methods for juveniles or people who are not mentally inclined to understand the law. However, cases where false confessions are made due to the misuse of Reid methods must indicate an exoneration. If an individual consistently proclaim their innocence, interrogators continue to question suspects for several hours causing fatigue, anxiety, and nervousness which can ultimately lead to false confessions. Future research should further emphasize how Reid tactics can be harmful to juveniles and people with mental disabilities. Law enforcement must improve their interviewing skills when questioning youth due to the underlying perception that children and adults process things the same way. Research supports overall, they do not.

In peroration, it is critical that stereotypes and racial biases do not get in the way of prosecutor discretion, sentencing, and pretrial detention efforts for nonviolent offenders. Conducting a standard risk assessment that is suitable for the rich and the poor will alleviate overt bias in the criminal justice system. Although quarterly ethics training will be beneficial to prosecutors, attorneys, law enforcement, school resource officers, and judges, acknowledgment of such disparities is the most cost-effective in deterring systematic oppression in sentencing.

Law enforcement officers are the first criminal defense exposed to the public. When minorities distrust and become suspicious of law enforcement officers, the bridge between officers and the justice system are conflicting battles. To elevate trauma from sentencing disparities, law enforcement agencies must publicly proclaim that they are committed to taking a stand against racial and ethnic disparities in the criminal justice system.

The research proves that there is an intersectional common denominator that fuels racial disparities. The outcome of economic strain is experienced by those who are likely poor and minority. They are primarily impacted in pretrial detention because they do not have the resources to remain free until a trial date. Community resources such as social services, public assistance, and other community investments become vital in decision-making processes for pretrial detention. If a minority and a non-minority commit the same drug offense, the outcome can be different due to socio-economic class. Furthermore, it is imperative to examine outdated drug policies stemming from the war on drugs. The cost is free to do the right thing by bringing home mothers and fathers that are still behind bars from outdated drug policies proven not to be as effective.

Many Black Americans and Latinos are disadvantaged today, because of the racially motivated policies that targeted them. The collateral damages ex-offenders face is too significant, restoring driver's license privileges, public assistance, and financial aid towards a new trade skill would also improve recidivism and sentencing disparities in non-violent offenders.

It is beneficial to non-violent offenders for the state of Virginia, or any other state, to level the playing field by enforcing the elimination of excessive bail amounts. Poverty should not be criminalized based on employment and an offender's ability to pay. Through detailed risk assessments and release conditions, non-violent offenders will have the opportunity to be free until convicted in a trial without the hassle of facing punishment for being too needy and Black. There are other alternatives to sentencing poor non-violent offenders before a trial date. The alternatives are pretrial supervision, frequent drug testing, behavioral health treatment, travel restrictions, the surrender of all travel documents, electronic monitoring, and curfew. These should be taken into consideration after a thorough risk assessment compiled from legitimate research, instead of mere computerized algorithms.

The best way to challenge an unjust law is to create a petition by demanding the revocation of excessive cash bail for non-violent offenders and ascertaining the number of signatures required to put the action on the ballot. The trajectory of deterring bias in sentencing non-violent offenders is well-defined in the previous discussion. The effectiveness of combating racial and ethnic sentencing disparities must be measured by examining the number of minorities vs. non-minorities incarcerated in pretrial detention for similar non-violent offenses, in comparison to those offenders who are jailed because they cannot afford bail. It is also critical that officials examine the bias algorithms used to determine risk factors favoring the majority. The disparities shown will reflect that poverty and race, not the level of danger, is a stipulation for why non-violent offenders are jailed until trial. Some may never see a day in court.

The goal is to eliminate cash bail for non-violent offenders. Judges must make sentencing determinations based on reliable risk assessments to weigh the possibility of an offender returning to prison. It should not be due to biased discretion or arbitrary stereotypes. Such a course of action in making determinations by way of detailed risk assessments, must be attainable for all justice systems across America without discrimination. Furthermore, every state and the federal institution must be on board with the same call to action regardless of social class and race.

Policy changes must be facilitated by evidence-based research provided in the discussion to address the issue of inequalities in prison sentencing. It is well-known that bad policies are caucused by media sources and other non-sequitur rhetoric such as the war on drugs and all that it entailed. Therefore, in uncovering the sentencing discrepancies, it is assumed that the cash bail system falls short of what it was intended to do, which was secure release from prison, and guarantee the offender's return to court. What happened to Kalief Browder is an example of structuralized racism is embedded in America's criminal justice system.

If socio-economic factors are indicators for law enforcement to stop Black and Latino citizens, eliminating excessive cash bail works. It can further deter pervasive racism in the form of sentencing within the criminal justice system. If risk assessments are utilized transparently, society can confront and combat racial disparities. Offenders should be able to appeal questionable risk assessments used by the court system to determine whether an offender goes to jail or not. Risk assessments should legitimately take into consideration an offender's criminal record, the nature of the charges, any prior failures to appear in court, employment history, and drug test results. Risk assessments should also further analyze where law enforcement heavily patrols as well as areas where law enforcement is scarce.

If offenders cannot make bail, they also lose their jobs, which is a repetitive cycle into poverty. Deficiency makes the cash bail system unreasonable. It is time to rethink sentencing for non-violent offenders.

"Change will not come if we wait for some other person or if we wait for some other time. We are the ones we've been waiting for. We are the change we seek."
Barack Obama

References

Agnew, R., & Brezina, T. (2015). Juvenile Delinquency: Causes and Control (Fifth ed.). New York: Oxford University Press

Baranauskas, A., & Drakulich, K. (2018). Media construction of crime revisited: Media types, consumer contexts, and frames of crime and justice. *Criminology*, 56(4), 679-714

Bleakley, P., & Bleakley, C. (2018). School resource officers, 'zero tolerance' and the enforcement of compliance in the American education system. *Interchange: A Quarterly Review of Education*, 49(2), 247-261. doi:10.1007/s10780-018-9326-5

Boyle, O., & Stanley, E. (2019). Private prisons and the management of scandal. *Crime, Media, Culture*, 15(1), 67-87

Campbell, C., Papp, J., Barnes, A., Onifade, E., & Anderson, V. (2018). Risk assessment and juvenile justice. *Criminology & Public Policy*, 17(3), 525–545

Campbell, N. A., Barnes, A. R., Mandalari, A., Onifade, E., Campbell, C. A., Anderson, V. R. & Davidson, W. S. (2018). Disproportionate minority contact in the juvenile justice system: An investigation of ethnic disparity in program referral at disposition. *Journal of Ethnicity in Criminal Justice*, 16(2), 77–98

Casey, B. J., Jones, R. M., & Somerville, L. H. (2011). Braking and accelerating of the adolescent brain. *Journal of Research on Adolescence* (Wiley-Blackwell), 21(1), 21–33

Cohen, A., & Casey, B. (2014). Rewiring juvenile justice: The intersection of developmental neuroscience and legal policy. *Trends in Cognitive Sciences*, 18(2), 63-5. Retrieved from https://doi:10.1016/j.tics.2013.11.002

COPS. (2016). How Mental Health Training Helps School Resource Officers. The e-newsletter of the COPS Office 9(2). Retrieved from https://cops.usdoj.gov/html/dispatch/022016/mental_health_and_sros.asp

Counts, J., Randall, K. N., Ryan, J. B., & Katsiyannis, A. (2018). School resource officers in public schools: A national review. *Education & Treatment of Children*, 41(4), 405–429

Death Penalty Information Center. (4 February 2020). Twenty-one Virginia prosecutors sign letter urging repeal of death penalty. Retrieved from https://deathpenaltyinfo.org/ news/twenty-one-virginia-prosecutors-sign-letter-urging-repeal-of-death-penalty

Dilulio, J. (1996). Fill Churches, Not Jails: Youth crime and "Superpredators". *Brookings*. Retrieved from https://www.brookings.edu/testimonies/fill-churches-not-jails-youth- crime-and-superpredators/

Donnelly, E. (2017). The disproportionate minority contact mandate: An examination of its impacts on juvenile justice processing outcomes (1997-2011). *Criminal Justice Policy Review*, 28(4), 347-369. doi:10.1177/0887403415585139

Drakulich, K. M., & Kirk, E. M. (2016). Public opinion and criminal justice reform. *Criminology & Public Policy*, 15(1), 171–177

Ewing, A. (2016). In/visibility: Solitary confinement, race, and the politics of risk management. *Transition*, (119), 109-123

Fischman, J. & Schanzenbach, M. (2012). Racial disparities under the federal sentencing guidelines: The role of judicial discretion and mandatory minimums. *Journal of Empirical Legal Studies*, 9(4), 729-764

Fry, A., O'Riordan, D., & Geanellos, R. (2002). Social control agents or front-line careers for people with mental health problems: Police and mental health services in Sydney, Australia. *Health & Social Care in the Community*, 10(4), 277-286. Retrieved from https://doi:10.1046/j.1365-2524.2002.00371.x

Geller, A., & Fagan, J. (2019). Police contact and the legal socialization of urban teens. *RSF: The Russell Sage Foundation Journal of the Social Sciences*, 5(1), 26-49

Gershowitz, A. M. (2016). Post-trial plea bargaining in capital cases: Using conditional clemency to remove weak cases from death row. *Washington & Lee Law Review*, 73(3), 1359-1394

Gottschalk, M. (2011). Extraordinary sentences and the proposed police surge. *Criminology & Public Policy*, 10(1), 123–136

Grommon, E. (2017). Public perceptions and housing assistance for reentrants. *Criminology & Public Policy*, 16(3), 827–833

Gross, S.R., Possley, M., & Stephens, K. (2017). Race and Wrongful convictions in the United States. Irvine, CA: The National Registry of Exonerations

Harper, C. C., & McLanahan, S. S. (2004). Father Absence and Youth Incarceration. *Journal of Research on Adolescence* (Wiley-Blackwell), 14(3), 369–397

Harris, L. (2015). New perspectives on criminal (in)justice and incarceration. *The Journal of African American History*, 100(3), 448-460

Hood, K., & Schneider, D. (2019). Bail and pretrial detention: Contours and causes of temporal and county variation. *RSF: The Russell Sage Foundation Journal of the Social Sciences*, 5(1), 126-149

Hurley, R., Jensen, J., Weaver, A., & Dixon, T. (2015). Viewer ethnicity matters: Black crime in tv news and its impact on decisions regarding public policy. *Journal of Social Issues*, 71(1), 155-170

Iratzoqui, A. (2018). Strain and opportunity: A theory of repeat victimization. *Journal of Interpersonal Violence,* 33(8), 1366-1387

Jackson, B., Russo, J., Hollywood, J., Woods, D., Silberglitt, R., Drake, G. & Chow, B. (2015). From corrections today to corrections tomorrow: Identifying needs in community and institutional corrections. In fostering innovation in community and institutional corrections: Identifying high-priority technology and other needs for the U.S. corrections sector (pp. 39-50). *RAND Corporation*

Jacobs, D., Qian, Z., Carmichael, J.T., & Kent, S. (2007). Who survives on death row? An individual and contextual analysis. *American Sociological Review*, 72(4), 610-632

Jacobs, D., Carmichael, J.T. & Kent, S.L. (2005). Vigilantism, current racial threat, and John DiIulio's plan to counter the "super-predators" of the inner city

Johnson, B.D., Stewart, E.A. Pickett, J., & Gertz, M. (2011). Ethnic threat and social control: Examining public support for judicial use of ethnicity in punishment *Criminology*, 49(2), 401-441. doi:10.1111/j.1745-9125.2011.00225.x

Jones, M. (2016). A Bronx tale: Disposable people, the legacy of slavery, and the social death of Kalief Browder. *University of Miami Race & Social Justice Law Review*, 6(1)

Kahn, K. B., & Martin, K. D. (2016). Policing and race: Disparate treatment, perceptions, and policy responses. *Social Issues & Policy Review*, 10(1), 82–121

Kovandzic, T., Sloan, J., & Vieraitis, L. (2002). Unintended consequences of politically popular sentencing policy: The homicide promoting effects of "three strikes" in U.S. cities (1980- 1999). *Criminology & Public Policy*, 1(3), 399-424

Kovera, M. B. (2019). Racial disparities in the criminal justice system: Prevalence, causes, and a search for solutions. *Journal of Social Issues*, 75(4), 1139-1164

Levine, K. L. & Wright, R. F. (2017). Prosecutor risk, maturation, and wrongful conviction practice. *Law & Social Inquiry*, 42(3), 648-676

Longazel, J. (2013). Subordinating myth: Latino/a immigration, crime, and exclusion. *Sociology Compass*, 7(2), 87-96

Mack, K., Jones, C., & Ballesteros, M. (2017). Illicit drug use, illicit drug use disorders, and drug overdose deaths in metropolitan and nonmetropolitan areas - United States. *Morbidity and Mortality Weekly Report. Surveillance Summaries* (Washington, D.C.:2002), 66(19), 1-2

Mahoney, A. R. (1981). Family participation for juvenile offenders in deinstitutionalization programs. *Journal of Social Issues*, 37(3), 133–144.

Mallett C. A. (2017). The school-to-prison pipeline: Disproportionate impact on vulnerable children and adolescents. *Education and Urban Society* 49(6):563– 92

McLaughlin, E., Savidge, M. & Sanchez, R. (5 March 2020). Nathanial Woods: Alabama executes inmate. *CNN*. Retrieved from https://www.cnn.com/2020/03/05/us/alabama-nathaniel-woods execution/index.html.

Meyer, J.R., & Reppucci N. D. (2007). Police practices and perceptions regarding juvenile interrogation and interrogative suggestibility. *Behavior Sciences and the Law*, 25, 757- 780

Mitchell, O., Cochran, J., Mears, D., & Bales, W. (2017). The effectiveness of prison for reducing drug offender recidivism: a regression discontinuity analysis. *Journal of Experimental Criminology*, 13(1), 1–27

Mondak, J., Hurwitz, J., Peffley, M., & Testa, P. (2017). The Vicarious Bases of Perceived Injustice. *American Journal of Political Science*, 61(4), 804-819

Munn, M. (2011). Living in the aftermath: The impact of lengthy incarceration on post-carceral success. *The Howard Journal of Criminal Justice*, 50(3), 233-246

NASTRO. (2014). The National Association of School Resource Officers. Retrieved from https://nasro.org/cms/wp-content/uploads/2014/04/AMHT-SRO-Course-Outline-and-Objectives.pdf

Nathan, D. (2016). What happened to Sandra Bland? *Nation*, 302(19/20), 12–18

Paresky, M. L. (2017). Changing welfare as we know it, again: Reforming the welfare reform act to provide all drug felons access to food stamps. *Boston College Law Review*, 58(5), 1659–1697

Parker, K.F., Stults, B., & Rice, S.K. (2005). Racial threat, concentrated disadvantage and social control: Considering the macro-level sources of variation in arrests. *Criminology*, 43(4), 1111-1134. doi:10.1111/j.1745-9125.2005.00034

Pearse, J. (1995). Police interviewing: The identification of vulnerabilities. *Journal of Community & Applied Social Psychology*, 5(3), 147–159

Pentek, C., & Eisenberg, M. (2018). School resource officers, safety, and discipline: Perceptions and experiences across racial/ethnic groups in Minnesota secondary schools. *Children and Youth Services Review*, 88, 141-148. https://doi:10.1016/j.childyouth.2018.03.008

R. v. Thaher, ONCJ 113 (2016) Retrieved from https://www.canlii.org/en/on/oncj/doc/2016/2016oncj113/2016oncj113.html

Rehavi, M., & Starr, S. (2014). Racial disparity in federal criminal sentences. *Journal of Political Economy*, 122(6), 1320-1354

Rhineberger-Dunn, G., Briggs, S., & Rader, N. (2016). Clearing crime in prime-time: The disjuncture between fiction and reality. American *Journal of Criminal Justice*, 41(2), 255–278

Rickford, R. (2016). Black lives matter. New Labor Forum (Sage Publications Inc.), 25(1), 34– 42

Roberts, B., & Chen, Y. (2013). Drugs, Violence, and the State. *Annual Review of Sociology*, 39, 105-125.

Romero, R. D., & McEwen, B. S. (2006). Stress and the adolescent brain. *Annals of the New York Academy of Sciences*, 1094(1), 202–214

Rosino, M., & Hughey, M. (2018). The war on drugs, racial meanings, and structural racism: A holistic and reproductive approach. *American Journal of Economics and Sociology*, 77(3- 4), 849-892

Rusby, J. C., Crowley, R., Sprague, J., & Biglan, A. (2011). Observations of the middle school environment: The context for student behavior beyond the classroom. *Psychology in the Schools*, 48(4), 400–415

Selman, D., & Leighton, P. (2010). Punishment for sale: private prisons, big business, and the incarceration binge. Rowman & Littlefield Publishers

Simmons, C., Steinberg, L., Frick, P., & Cauffman, E. (2018). The differential influence of absent and harsh fathers on juvenile delinquency. *Journal of Adolescence*, 62, 9-17

Stanley, J (2015). The War on Thugs: How propaganda fuels our prison system. *The Chronical Review.* Retrieved from https://www.chronicle.com/article/The-War-on-Thugs/230787

The Office of Juvenile Justice and Delinquency Prevention. (2018). Statistical Briefing Book. Law Enforcement and Juvenile Crime. Juvenile Arrest Rate Trends. Retrieved from http://www.ojjdp.gov/ojstatbb/crime/JAR_Display.asp?ID=qa05200&selOffenses=1. October 22, 2018

Turney, K., & Schneider, D. (2016). Incarceration and household asset ownership. *Demography*, 53(6), 2075-2103

Unnever, J.D., & Cullen, F.T. (2010). The social sources of Americans' punitiveness: A test of three competing models. *Criminology*, 48(1), 99-129

Vrij, A. (2008). Detecting lies and deceit: Pitfalls and opportunities (2nd ed). Chichester, UK: Wiley and Sons, Inc

Westervelt, S. D., & Cook, K. J. (2018). Continuing trauma and aftermath for exonerated death row survivors. In H. Toch, J. R. Acker, & V. M. Bonventre (Eds.), Living on death row: The psychology of waiting to die (pp. 301-329). Washington, DC, US: American Psychological Association

Woodruff, M. (2013). The excessive bail clause: Achieving pretrial justice reform through incorporation. *Rutgers Law Review, 66*(1), 241-297

Yang, C. (2017). Does public assistance reduce recidivism? *The American Economic Review*, 107(5), 551-555

Yates, J., & Whitford, A. (2009). Race in the war on drugs: The social consequences of presidential rhetoric. *Journal of Empirical Legal Studies*, 6(4), 874-898

Zinger, I. (2012). Conditional release and human rights in Canada: A commentary. *Canadian Journal of Criminology & Criminal Justice*, 54(1), 117–135. Retrieved from https://doi- org.saintleo. idm.oclc.org/10.3138/cjccj.2011.E.19